I

Suffered Truth is Sundered Youth

Bleeding hearts soon break apart

The burning can be buffered out

But truth leaves lingering scars;

Are we naught but kindred dead

Soon bleed and end up dead

Alone forsaken on bird's owed wing

Debt to pay in death o'er sting;

Utopia is a burnished dream

That drowns in the fear of dead thing's deeds;

Of bleeding crown and blood stained gems

None to bore the savior's throne.

II

We walk in tortured paths of hate

Of woe born fear

None lies down with Iota's aid

O' there be nothing that can bend

Behind Iota's violet shield

Ionized atoms sing in glorious symphony

Defending all those shieldless

Eternal blazes fear single droplets

The world's greatest warrior

Fears naught but the world's worst.

III

Tears shed for broken gods

Arn't but fearless prose;

Few can flee the o'er looming shadow

That is the first's ugly head

In the death throes of the Universe

O' Pestilence, thou shaken spear

Dissolves and climbs through

Veins and bogs

IV

And in some small way, I know what's happening to me.

I can see it bubbling to fruition before me

And yet, I am powerless to stop it.

Suffice to say, I have fallen hopelessly in love.

V

What a grotesque word

"love"

4 letters with a billion meanings.

Yet here I am feeling it.

I'm furiously mad at myself

I'm a hypocrite

No way around it

I detested love and relationships

"waste of time

sundered conscience"

I had said

and yet

and yet I made her the exception to the rule

Why did I do that?

I'm not sure, entirely.

VI

It's been a very long while

Since I've felt such things in my bones

Such harmony resonating in my soul

It's odd

It feels odd

and yet so very beautiful and perfect

Like acid in my veins, blood in my mouth

All irony and burning sensations

VII

Happy is something I find peculiar.

Another of the things I have not felt in a period of time

And yet, now all things are consumed in this golden haze

All I want for her is

"happy"

Her smile is something meek and warm. I adore it.

I am however saddened that I will never be able to describe her un-objectively

The rose colored lenses have replaced my corneas.

All I hear is roaring music in everything

The way she looks at me melts my heart

Molten steel cast in the shape of "whatever she wants"

VIII

I hate what I've become

And yet I don't despise the notion

What a name

What a face

What a smile

and eyes like the sun reflecting off metal

Fleeting and wondrous to those unaccustomed to the idea.

IX

I should probably be sleeping right now, but I am oh so terribly inspired at the moment. I have inadvertently invoked a muse that goes by the name of a flower and is the incarnation of fall and beauty. I am a Gemini, a two sided coin, irreversibly torn between morals and efficiency. I stay

here, writing in prose.

And sometimes not since the great old Bard

Believes madness is associated with coherent thought

Though, there is an irony in that all.

Alas, I am hypnotized by a woodland faerie

I still feel her lips on mine

Lighting and warmth

She has me confused in a way I have not been for o so very long

Our lips clash like lovers

Like how summer waves break against the beach

Like how dolphins breach

With the grace of an owl snatching prey from

The holy Earth

X

The Bard inquires as to the contents of a name

I reply in a soliloquy of my choosing

He is appeased and she blushes

Lily

Sketches of beautiful, freckled girls

Warm cups of tea and nostalgia

Soft everything and warm skies

Contrasted by cold temperatures and darkness

Death's abode mocked by Aphrodite's

Tender are the hands that guide these hands

All at once I am fearful and ignorant

Complacent and wondrous as to the world around me

For once, this old twin feels as though he as changed

And, for once, the world didn't change with him

Yet it is now tinted with sunlight and the autumnal gratification that comes with those months

I am all hard steel and she is hot coffee

We both reach for the same things though

"Art for art's sake" I say

She says nothing and laughs

I secretly hope she doesn't/does/won't ever/ agree with me

XI

I am not ignorant to facts

I know this type of thing rarely works out

I'd be waiting two years for her

Two years of odd looks from others or no direct communication

I'm thinking so far ahead, not knowing if everything will end tomorrow

Death looms overhead

He watches me type, bones creaking with oddity.

I have avoided him at every pass, yet I know his scythe to be at my neck always and never

Paradoxical

I wish I could talk to him

Sit down for coffee and ask how long

And for more time if the previous answer doesn't satisfy me

Because for once, I am not infatuated with purely the physical, like it has been before.

No, I have fallen in love with a voice like Bourbon over ice

With a smile made of young maple

With eyes that reach into my soul and drag my heart kicking and screaming from its cage

I am hostage

I am Stockholm in love with an endlessly fascinating mind

And she?

She is a Libra that denies me sadness

In the absence of failure, I am left alone with pride and dignity

And that dreadful love that eats everything ugly

All that remains is pure

Happy

That's a word I haven't been able to say in quite sometime

I want this to work out

I want to go to New York with her

I want to take the stage with her

I want Broadway in our hands as our lips touch

I care very little for the fleeting

For the ephemeral

Always concerned with my legacy and my work

Leaving behind a trove of art that exists to inspire further works

I would love to die and be resurrected as a muse

Yet, I fear she may be nothing more than a passing glance

I'm afraid that if I stop looking, she won't be there when I turn back

XII

I acknowledge the risks

The "La folie des amoureux"

The bravery required to love that which is not forever

To place value in something you cannot always have with you

I acknowledge and accept

Stolen Truth is Somehow Youth

XIII

My muse makes my heart beat terribly fast

Music races through my veins

And mine head fills with beauty

She is intoxicatingly beautiful

And I, I am but a thing she compares to a tree in fall

The taste of her lips

The smell of her perfume

The way she moans into my mouth

The way she kisses my neck

There's is a rough beauty in freshly kindled romance

Sprouting from the Earth and falling irreversibly in love with the sun

Leaves turned towards heaven and peace

Its roots in Satan's realm, but its face towards God's

She sets my soul ablaze like Moses' bush

XIV

I h've lost all rhyme

Alas, outrun from time

It's horrid march

It's horrid march

It's horrid march dost spark my heart

Her fingers are jumper cables

Her heart, a battery full of life

And mine, one dead

XV

Sometimes I get that 1000 yard stare

I get lost in a moment of lucidity

It's as if everything up until than was just a dream

I get caught up in/with?/until that moment

A lifetime of living catches up with me in an instant

I am blind sided by this sudden clarity

It passes, though

In time, everything does.

I pray that my love for Her, however, does not ever falter

Does not ever fade

She is everything to me

Symbolic of my sanity as I force lines through my finger tips

I'm not sure if she understands

I am not entirely sure that even I understand

She is so pure and precious to me

I do not wish to be the gardener snake to her Eve

It is not my wish to open her eyes to worlds beyond her knowledge

Worlds that wish to horridly corrupt her soul

Boil it in turmoil\

But it is my fetish, is it not?

Corruption

To taint flesh with fear and hate and lust

I am the snake

I am the devil

In one way or another

I am poison into the veins of innocence

Stories and actions are my fangs

I am a serpent of/

She used to write poetry and draw those that were with her romantically

She says she stopped because it created unrealistic expectations

Alas, what did I expect?

A woman that romanticized romance until she hated it

I am enthralled

Tantalized

A step upon which I must fall down, or else, o'erleap

To have her write about me

That is my Prince of Cumberland

To have her draw me

That is my King Duncan

And my tempting lust for more than just flesh

That is my Birnam Wood on its way to Dunsinane

She is my Scottish crown

My throne that I have risked everything for

My throne that I will risk everything for

My throne that I risked everything for

I am full of doubt and love

I believe her to be filled with as much

Perhaps more

I am confused and scared

My mind torn in places I didn't know as such

XVI

I am a fox caught in a gale

And I have never felt so safe

XVII

I am a frog in a boiling pot

And there is nothing that can save me now

XVIII

She is my Judas

Her kiss damns me

Yet she makes my soul sing like harmonious fire

Burning suns and liquid heat

I am fearful

I am brave

I am paradoxical in nature

And hypocritical in action

My heart hurts

She makes me hurt in perfect bliss

Painless nature is fretful

Painful presence is a sign of life

Of living

Of loving

XIX

Glass spiders skip across fields of barley

I am the Shepard of impossibilities

My mind a world-scape

Mine eyes bleed liquid glass 'cross all realities

Tinging and warping modern day to the ridiculous

Are we not all gods, in our own regards?

If not to ourselves, to others?

I know I worship her, pledge myself at an altar that I don't understand

XX

I am lucid

Living a dream that is not of my own creation

I am surrounded by a thousand legs

Arachnids march to a stolen beat

Around my head

I am resolved

Fear and love, two halves of one coin

They are so remarkably close,

That I often cannot distinguish between the two

Maybe the middle ground is respect

The material of the coin

Love. the inscribed face

Fear, the detailed insignia

And I am all at once.

XXI

I consider the future

What will happen in the "After-Death"

Where all things end and begin

At least, that's how they see it

The Great Mob

They believe high school is the end of childhood

The beginning of adulthood

I beg to differ

Those are but states of mind determined by behavior

Neither ends or begins as soon as the diploma touches your hands

Adulthood is simply forgoing creative freedom, accepting mediocrity

Discrediting everyone that helped you climb to where you are now

Insulting all those whose shoulders you stand on

Childhood is living in endless wonder and immaturity

Both I hate

Yet, I will carve a path on each side of the road

I will toe the line

Live how I want to live, regardless of what The Great Mob thinks

Iota guides me, protects me.

Guardian of the shieldless is my own shield

I am a Gemini

Materialistic but not

Hateful of the philosophy that I o' so admire

XXII

All I want to is create

To be God in my own respect

These passages shall be my Adam and Eve

My other works, my Moses and Abraham

We were made in our creator's own image

So is there no irony in wanting to create for ourselves?

Religion is propaganda

Faith is entrapment

And yet there is an uneasy beauty in the idea of something grand with massive hands

Culling our consciousness for eternity

Ribs and mud

There is a reliability in pre-destination

The idea that everything is already set to happen, that there is no way around it

It is a gentle ideal, for gentle souls

I reject it completely

To water down consequences

To make them seem as if they're unavoidable is stupidity incarnate

Consequences are real

True maturity is accepting them for all they are

Admitting your follies and living with it

So Their Snakes Yearn

Serpentine blood filtered through

A pair of old eye glasses

A yellowed novel, driving young men insane

Crimson sheen on emerald jade

The poor, old God

The old, poor God

Aristotle on the streets

Bargaining with patriotism, betrayals of the homeland

Great anthems for dying soldiers

Bleeding fronds

Scarlet and tangential, as is all that is unreal

I am a poet submerged in ice

My spinal fluid frozen

The blood in my brain thickens like molasses

But, alas, I have thawed

I gasp for breath, ignorant of how my surroundings have changed

Or perhaps not

Perhaps I am the only one that noticed the change

The steely azures are now tinted

With pale golds and violets

Iota walks past me

Iota grabs my hand and leads me towards the sun

Like the wax figurine of Greek origin and irony

I melt

And I am happy

What a word

What a feeling

XXIII

I wish, like all great artists,

To be like the avians

Feathered beasts that own the sky

All hollow bones and fleeting beauty

I wish to burn brightly like a candle at both ends

Then to bleed out into obscurity

Now, o'er one half world

Nature seems dead and

Nothing

Nothing

Nothing quite burns like clockwork

Like old wood and burnished copper

Like brains born of hate and deception

We are all Bards in our own regards

We all feel sunlight off o' cool steel

I wish for perfect Harmony

I wish for death to lay down next to me

My lover eyeing my muse

My muse eyeing my lover

I have not decided which is which

Nor if they be each other

One and the same

She is my death

My perfect, eternal bliss

She is all I fear and love and respect

She is the coin and I am the one that holds it

Or perhaps not

Perhaps it is the other way around

Sometimes I believe that

Sometimes I reject

Or accept

Freedom stolen, but it feels as though I hath given it away'

There are only so many gifts that have meaning in my eyes

So I give her my free will,

In sacrifices I dream

Perhaps she gave it back?

Slipped it into my pocket whilst I was distracted

My work overcomes mine senses

Iota laughs, she knows I don't need her

I reassure her that I do

I compose a symphony in her honor but the look remains

Imbedded in her eyes like a tattoo upon porcelain flesh

maybe i'm just crazy

XXIV

Hate

What a word

What a feeling

Something I cannot attach to her, regardless of how hard I try

I don't think I hate anything

Though I believe I hate everything

Existence is pain through which hope is born

We are its womb

We birth hope through our voices and hands and eyes and tongues and teeth and fingers and

We who stand apart from The Great Mob

We who deny those Suffered Truths

We who deny those Stolen Yellow flowers

We are all star dust and carbon

Youthful ignorance made from the unplayable symphony

Despised by death

Us fearless few

Though I don't believe I belong with them

Nor The Great Mob

I am alone on an island

Denying ideologies and fearing Death

Iota can't protect me now

If she ever did

XXV

Iota

The Nth

IX

She has many names

I do not know what she represents

If she's even real

Who or what

But I see her when I close my eyes

Her eyes stare into mine

Perhaps she is my guardian angel

Protecting

Or perhaps not,

Perhaps she is my own personal devil

A demon

A phantom

Iota scares me

I am frightened

XXVI

Together we stand

From here, the stars

From here, we promise to heal all Denizens of the World

From here, we will make the weak strong

We will build monuments

We will bleed dry the nay sayers

There are no mountains I cannot climb

There are no heavens I cannot grasp

There is nothing

Everything can fade

Alone, I fall

XXVII

I see it everywhere

A billion slivers of cobblestone embedded in my jaw

A trillion drops of blood running along the grooves in my finger tips

XXVIII

I wish to be like fleece

I wish to be like rain

I wish to be like nails on a chalkboard

I wish to be like white hot nails cascading to the floor

Sparks on impact

Music obscured by a deafening cacophony

I wish to dream a thousand dreams that I never remember'

It is foolish

Extremely foolish to place value in the ephemeral

In the temporary pleasures, but to not is to give in to nihilism

You must enjoy the small things, o' reader mine

Lest insanity take hold and eat away at the meat sweet mortality

The blood soaked humanity

The singing of cardinals on a thousand corpses

XXIX

I drank from the fountain once

Youth

What a word

What a face

Something I hate to envy

And I envy it with hate

To care very little for beauty

That is what I believe creates beauty

To put no purchase in my art is what makes it precious

I make my art for no one but me

And that is why these pages will live forever

I, in turn, will with it

My ideals will be stained into the minds of a billion

And that is immortality

That is legacy and beauty in my eyes

I yearn for those long, slow days.

I live for the terror in the streets

I thrive in blissful horror

I strive for arrogant deaths

I wish to be like nothing

I wish to be like no one

Words will not contain me

Words will not consume/constrain me

I am not a passage of text

I am not definable by lyrics

I am an indescribable terror

Or, at least that's what I wish to be like

XXX

I want to live forever

And forever

And always

I want to give and give

Create and create

Until existence itself bends to my whim

Till I can stare some starry eyed monstrosity down

Till I can taste the cosmos and paint it on a canvas

There is an indescribable impunity that comes with understanding

I wish to know everything

Yet knowing nothing is easier on the heart

I will torture myself in the name of hellfire

Forged and renewed in the heat of sound

Of neutrons firing and protons singeing/singing

Burnt toast and alchemical reactions

XXXI

I have fallen in love with a meteor

I know it will kill me but there is a certain beauty in those final moments

Clarity.

XXXII

Moths with dusty wings

Serene oceans of nitrogen

Freezing

Burning

Metaphorically speaking

We're all every nothing there isn't

Opal beauty in obsidian glass

I fear the beauty that thaws my stolen/broken/sundered heart

I'm torn between two greater evils for her

Love and fear

Coins go in circles

Criminals proven innocent

Cycled laundry

XXXIII

I tear apart

The sudden admiration I momentarily feel

The destruction of something I had so soon created

The enticing phantasmal

XXXIV

I wish I could stop with this self-aware pseudo-nonsense. I wish I could write and make sense, I know I can. I did. I already have but I want more, I want my sparks of inspiration to kindle bonfires. I want them to burn for eons as I cook words in them, stoke the fire with paint brushes, breath in the smoke and exhale lyrical magic. I wish—no I want to be the best that has ever existed. I want my works to make people laugh at Shakespeare, mock Mozart, and find Van Gogh boring. I'm disgusted with everything I've done so far. I'm a failure.

XXXV

I bleed poetry

I scream musicals

I break into a thousand, billion, trillion pieces

There is nothing left

nothing left

nothing left

but nothing is right

Everything feels raw and immovable

A wall before me

It extends as far as I can see

The invisible horizon

Hidden behind barbed wire and

Mirrored lies

I dream in crystalline moods and seeded consciousness

Doubt

We have no room for such a thing

Keep the bastard buried under rocks

O' foul hearted stealer of potential

Fear hath no place in mine heart,

Yet I invite in its fair sister,

Residence in which it takes up

Is full of nothing but buried doubt

Bloodied knuckles and metamorphic rock

Blades of grass hug my feet

Iota may meet me on the other side

O'er else there is nothing worth staying

For time bleeds faster in the places it tastes the worst

XXXVI

I don't want to show her,

What is here is so personal

Too much of myself in it's face

But part of me knows it was written for her,

Even if I didn't know it, even before we were together

This is for her

It feels as though ever step is for her

Wether I want it or not

I've made a deal with a devil, in exchange for an angel.

XXXVII

My soul thrives in these words,

Phrases made of sinew and bloody bits

XXXVIII

My biggest fear is her hate

Her

Her

Her

Her

Her

Her that's all I feel

That's all I see

Not the trillion gnashing teeth beneath my eyes

Not Iota's behind them

You must understand, the fragility of everything

Nothing is stable

Nothing is permanent

We are all dust in the wind

Winding roads and coins coinciding with rain clouds

Ionized hell in the distance

But we cannot taste it

The fine mist

Severed souls

Powdered death

Mold burnt with the musty basement with the whole house

All consuming

All purifying

Fire

In the sky the Mother Fire presides over existence

Extant and bloodied is the Earth

Her breathing shallow

But still living

Still fighting

Then still

Unmoving and curdled stillness

Like lumps in your throat

Glass in your veins

Metal in your eyes'

Titanium bones and fist sized hale

Rising sun fighting the gale

XXXIX

I am nothing but my art

I am nothing but love doused with gasoline

And set a blaze with a match called insanity and

What a perfect match we are

Together in blazing heat

I see faces all around me

I hear voices that aren't there

I am never/always alone

Painful tears

Tears in the fabric of reality

Death is but a memory of fear

A feeling of love

His teeth chatter

I'm not sure he can speak but I hear him still

Here and there in echoes of stillness

Uneasy speakers

Unfeeling terror

Blood shot eyes and inspired youths

A nation of such beasts

A kind of desire a planet can feed on

Can voraciously consume

XL

A system of nerves Scream

I knew him back then'

When he was but a boy

Before war chewed him up and spit him out

He just wasn't there anymore

After that

He just wasn't there anymore

After that

He just wasn't there anymore

After that

His eyes were empty like a doll

Opal darkness reflected in obsidian glass

So young

Such youth

Such wasted potential they'd say

Poor soul

On the streets

Freezing and dying like fireflies

When July turns to August

When leaves curl and dry and die

XLI

In the end

I fear nothing but her hate

I'm afraid that I will make her hate me

I make everyone hate me

It's my talent, I turn those I love against me

I've done it before, evidence suggests I'll do it again

This is my obituary.

My final statement

My wondrous final destination

XLII

I am lost and found again,

Billions of line tear through my scalp

Tears well in my eyes

Buckets bringing up pitchers of silver

Liquid silvers but it's not hot

I want to be it

Embody it

Deadly but incredible

Terrible wilderness

Tearable banners

Weaved to be broken

Snipped with big gold scissors

Unveiled destinations and silver cities

Silver screen and tiny boats

Soldiers draped in gold

mors pacificae

Oceans drowning out the lights and sights

Sounds all around

Putrid and imperfect

Please God forgive me

But I don't need his forgiveness

It matters very little what my cosmic creator believes of me

I am my own specimen

My own champion

I walk empty handed through hell and back

Fearful players fret upon a stage

Then are heard no longer

We are actors made for scenes of varying lengths

Secular in purpose

Impossible in detail

Torrential in meaning

XLIII

The lumpenproletariat that feasts on the dreams of the wicked

Thriving in oppression

Living for the destruction of the individual

The sleeper cell that balances all powers

The great equalizer'

I despise it all

I reject the theory

I falter in place, worlds/words failing on my lips

Mist to be dispersed like clouds

Ever present but always fleeting

Dying on the head of a needle

Failing to rouse enough suspicion to warrant an investigation

Open and closed

Cut and dry

The ol' cut and run

Great whirlwinds make us abandon our homes

I am a genius trapped in the mind of an idiot

I am pretentiously ignorant to the point of absurdity

Where do I end and where do you begin

Voices in your head in my voice

Squeaking like mice

Chattering like rats

Hordes and kings will rise and fall before any of this makes sense

Houses and banners

Gods and old men

Women and children

Failure is something I don't remember but will always regret

Stolen Teeth and Speech is Youthful/

Lack of teeth can't be useful/

But of broken bones and stolen souls

Electricity is what I pick

Fleeting neurology

Nerves made of flayed copper

Grounded pains and voltage galore

The all-knowing herald of gore

I write and I write and it all means something

I write and I write and I'm still nothing

Nothing except flesh and blood, gone in a 100 years

I am a sparkler on the 4th of July in my own mouth

I see spiders breathing

Silken, gossamer threads of life

Hades' web of crimson joy

Fearful fretting for all mortal glee

Nonsensical addresses in an imaginary book at the back of an imaginary closet in the home of some girl that isn't real and she never was but I still think she's alive and I've resorted to making her fiction because the truth is I miss her and I don't know where she went I'm too afraid to

accept the truth she's dead and I have survivor's guilt

Iota

I think that's her name

It is now

I have exhumed her corpse, sat her upright in my mind and gave her a shield to watch over me

I call her Iota 'cause it reminds me of her

Of long car rides and a deep violet

It's been so long

She was such a dear soul

And now she's gone

But never forgotten

She protects me now, like she did back then

IX is alive and well

Protector of all those that can't protect themselves

God save us all from ourselves

Knowing full well that our destruction will crescendo

We'll die at Fortissimo

The world at a Fortepiano.

And it all tastes like french bread.

www.ingramcontent.com/pod-product-compliance
Lightning Source LLC
Chambersburg PA
CBHW031515210526
45464CB00007B/2930